W9-DEM-280

LIFE CONFESSIONS

The Power of Your Words

Personal Prayers for Health, Wealth, Strength, and Freedom!

David R. White

All Scripture quotations are from the New King James Version of the Bible unless otherwise referenced.

LIFE CONFESSIONS

ISBN 1-512304-10-7

Copyright © 2015 David White

Cover Design: David White

P.O. Box 2202, Costa Mesa, CA 92628

All rights reserved

Manufactured in the United States of America

LIFE
CONFESSIONS

The Power of Your Words
Personal Prayers for Health, Wealth, Strength, and Freedom!

David R. White

CONTENTS

LIFE CONFESSIONS

INTRODUCTION

This book is a compilation of scriptural prayers, proclamations, and declarations designed to simplify and enhance your personal or corporate prayer time and easily enable you to speak out the Word of God over your life, family, friends, business, calls, mantles, anointings, dreams, and visions!

I hope you will enjoy these Life Confessions as much as I have enjoyed the fruit and fun of them in my life and ministry. Please feel free to make them your own and modify them to fit your life. I believe they will be a catalyst that will propel you into deeper revelation and inspiration through the power of the Holy Spirit! Get ready for breakthroughs and fresh testimonies of God's power and provision! He is Faithful!

Chapter 1

PAULINE PRAYERS

These Prayers are taken from the letters of Paul in the epistles and I have personalized them for you. I recommend that you speak them out loud, so that your own ears can hear the words that come from your mouth and out of your heart. I also recommend that you say them regularly and consistently because they will be transforming in your everyday life.

PRAYER POWER CONTINUALLY COMES OUT OF YOUR MOUTH THROUGH CONSTANT CONFESSION!

Ephesians 1:17-20

"...that You, the God of my Lord Jesus Christ, the Father of glory, may give to me the spirit of wisdom and revelation in the knowledge of You, the eyes of my understanding being enlightened; that I may know what is the hope of Your calling, what are the riches of the glory of Your inheritance in my life, and what is the exceeding greatness of Your power towards me who believes, according to the working of Your mighty power which You worked in Christ when You raised Him from the dead and seated Him at Your right hand in the heavenly places..."

Ephesians 3:14-21

"...I bow my knees to You, the Father of my Lord Jesus Christ, from whom the whole family in heaven and earth is named, that You would grant me, according to the riches of Your glory, to be strengthened with might through Your Spirit in my inner man, that Christ may dwell in my heart through faith; that I, being rooted and grounded in love, may be able to comprehend with all the saints what is the width, and length, and depth, and height; to know the love of Christ which passes knowledge; that I may be filled with all the fullness of God. Now to You, who is able to do exceedingly abundantly above all that I ask or think, according to the power that works in me, to You be glory in the church by Christ Jesus to all my generations, forever and ever. Amen."

Colossians 1:9-14

"Father, I ask that I may be filled with the knowledge of Your will in all wisdom and spiritual understanding; that I may walk worthy of You Lord, fully pleasing You, being fruitful in every good work and increasing in the knowledge of You; strengthened with all might, according to Your glorious power, for all patience and longsuffering with joy; giving thanks to the Father who has qualified me to be a partaker of the inheritance of the saints in the light. You have delivered me from the power of darkness and conveyed me into the kingdom of the Son of Your love, in whom I have redemption through Your blood, the forgiveness of all my sins."

Philippians 1:9-11

"And this I pray, that my love may abound still more and more in knowledge and all discernment, that I may approve the things that are excellent, that I may be sincere and without offense till the day of Christ, being filled with the fruits of righteousness which are by Jesus Christ, to the glory and praise of God."

Romans 15:5, 6, 13

"Now may You, the God of patience and comfort grant me to be like-minded toward others, according to Christ Jesus, that I may, with one mind and one mouth, glorify the God and Father of my Lord Jesus Christ. Now may You, the God of hope fill me with all joy and peace in believing, that I may abound in hope by the power of the Holy Spirit."

2 Thessalonians 1:11, 12

"I pray always, that my God would count me worthy of this calling, and fulfill all the good pleasure of His goodness and the work of faith with power, that the name of my Lord Jesus Christ may be glorified in me, and me in Him, according to the grace of my God and the Lord Jesus Christ."

Hebrews 13:20, 21

"Now may the God of peace who brought up my Lord Jesus from the dead (with resurrection power), that great Shepherd of the sheep, through the blood of the everlasting covenant, make me complete in every good work to do Your will, working in me what is well pleasing in Your sight, through Jesus Christ, to whom be glory forever and ever. Amen."

Chapter 2
PERSONAL PRAYERS

Health Prayer Declarations

Father, I pray for health in my body and my spouse's body, in our children's bodies, and in their families. I say NO. No to sickness or disease, no tumors, no growths, no pain or infirmity, no cancer in our bodies, organs, blood, lymph, respiratory, or circulatory systems. No skin cancer, irritations or blemishes. No accidents of any kind. I plead the blood of Jesus, the blood of the everlasting covenant, over all of us. I draw a blood line and surround us with a blood hedge of protection and believe for complete, divine, and angelic protection and health over us! Every organ, muscle, and vein functions perfectly and the life of God flows through our bodies! Our blood, blood vessels, and veins are clean, clear, and pure; even from the marrow of our bones where the blood is produced and there is no plaque buildup in our veins or heart. No heart disease, muscle disease, or organ disease. No disease of any kind! No disorders, no syndromes, no lying symptoms of any kind. For we are redeemed from all the curses of the law, poverty, sickness, and death and live extremely healthy and wealthy lives, glorifying You in our bodies! We prosper in health, our souls prosper, and we're wealthy in our bodily and physical health and wellbeing! The same Spirit that raised Christ from the dead QUICKENS and gives LIFE to our mortal bodies and we are strong and healthy physically and sharp mentally in memory, wisdom, counsel, insight, and clarity both naturally and spiritually! You continually renew our youth like the eagles and we run without weariness! Thank You Lord for physical strength, stamina, energy, and vitality! I live and enjoy every day with divine and natural health!

Financial Prayer Declarations

I Pray for Financial increase. Money into our hands and into our accounts, both personally in my everyday life, in my business, and in my church, 10s of 1,000s and 100s of 1,000s of dollars... Millions of dollars Lord. Increase, growth, and expansion in every area of my life concerning money. I call in blessing and divine favor. I have favor with God and so I declare that I have favor with all! I have a spirit of giving and generosity and I enjoy giving, sowing, planting, and blessing as well as receiving abundantly and consistently! I call in good jobs, solid positions right here locally in my city and county and I walk in divine favor that causes raises, bonuses, and contracts, new business connections and relationships, productivity, sales, and revenue! Multiplication and expansion, the filling of natural and spiritual storehouses with wealth and resources, creating collection and distribution centers of wealth and productivity, creative and revelatory epicenters! Birthing the new, the fresh, from Heaven to Earth! Revelatory and revolutionary! It's Jubilee time, all debts wiped out, the erasing and eradicating of all debt! Complete release from the master of debt and all its enslaving power and the income and provision to wipe it out and keep it out! Money is a slave to us, not our Master! Complete mindset changes. No poverty mindsets or poverty spirits, be loosed and be gone! I break, sever, and release the spirit of mammon and it's control in every form! We are free! Its overflow time, more than enough and abundance, a river and continuous supply of wealth and resources into our hands, into our accounts, and into our possession! No more waiting! No more delay! Patience has had her perfect work and I declare that we are complete and lacking nothing! The time is now. The fullness of time has come! The Spiritual and natural demand is pulling on the supply of Heaven! The supply is released to meet the demand! The wait is over! The supply will overtake the need and the dreams will be fulfilled! Abundant, surplus, overflow, increase, more than enough, bountiful, ample, plenty, excess, flourishing, multiplied, exponential, explosion, eruption, excess, extra... I am the God who is more than enough!

Breakthrough Prayer

It's freedom time! Jubilee! Release from all captivity, bondage, darkness, depression, oppression, addiction, and despair. Let the light shine! Break through the darkness with light and love. Natural and Supernatural favor right now, every day. Grace released, grace poured out on us all. An Open Heaven with blessings, graces, giftings, and divine abilities. Great Grace upon us Lord! I ask for your grace to help today, grace on me, grace on us, divine ability, and wisdom! Glorious inheritance and legacy, property and portion, heritage and ownership, prosperity and provision! Expected and unexpected gifts and surprises. Wealth transfer into our hands; money coming daily in the mail, over the internet, credit deposits, and handed to us as gifts that we receive with grateful and thankful hearts. Blessing bestowed on us and on all of my family with an eruption and explosion of growth and income in

17

our businesses, our homes, and personal lives! I believe for a surplus, extra, and overflow, more than enough with a consistent, constant flow! We are health and wealth magnets, attracting income, blessing, and favor. The right place at the right time, Kairos Time... "It is You who gives me power to get wealth, that You may establish Your covenant which You swore to our fathers, as it is this day." (Deut. 8:18 NKJV). And Father, I will remember You and acknowledge You in all this supply and provision, and recognize that You are the source of all we have and enjoy. Knowing You, experiencing You, and testifying out loud that all goodness, grace, and mercy comes from You! Divine wisdom and insight fills and floods my mind constantly and the Holy Spirit teaches and instructs me in everything that pertains to my daily life, calling, spiritual, and natural walk! Thank You Lord for the divine Shift, open doors, open gates, pathways, and avenues of freedom with Acceleration and Momentum! Accelerate into the blessing, vision, manifestation, fulfillment, and FUN in the Spirit and in the Natural! It's GO time! It's NOW time! No more delay! The wait is over! Come Forth! Be Released and Loosed into! And come upon! Into and upon! Falling and Filling in Jesus Name! Saturate, overtake, and overcome! Great Joy and Jubilation, excitement, gladness, happiness, and elation!

Revival and Awakening Prayer

Thank You Lord for increased anointings, abilities, and graces in my life and ministry; healings, miracles, deliverance, breakthroughs, restorations, greater manifested glory, angelic visitations, Salvations, SOZO, encounters, and open visions. Eyes and ears open to see, and hear, and know. Supernatural baptism with the Holy Ghost and Fire! The Word of the Lord, the Gift of Prophecy and the prophetic, the Apostolic, the Word of knowledge and Word of Wisdom, discerning of spirits, gifts of healings, the working of miracles, the Gift of Faith in operation, Holy Ghost Power, Dunamis Power, acceleration and momentum. More Lord, more. The right place at the right time, Kairos time, appointed time, and heavenly timings! COME AGAIN HOLY SPIRIT! Come in Power and great Glory! Come Holy Spirit, come! The beautiful, weighty, heavy presence of The Lord in our midst and in every meeting. Fill this house with your manifested presence, glory, and goodness. Shekinah glory; Heaven here now; Heaven's purity and grace! Blow upon us and bring the winds of revival and renewal, reformation, restoration, and creative renaissance! I call in the rain, the former and later rain together! Father, I thank You, and praise You, and give You all the glory for Your overflow of blessing, and health, and goodness in our lives and in all the individual lives, families, homes, and businesses of all that concern me! Oh Lord, You are great and greatly to be praised! Glory to God!

Thanksgiving Prayer

Out of the abundance of my heart my mouth speaks and I want to praise You and thank You Lord for who You are, for all that You Have done, and for all that You are doing in me and in and through my life! You are worthy, oh Lord, of all my worship and adoration and I will bless You and glorify Your Name all the days of my life!

Glory to God! Lord, You are my Rock, my Fortress, and my Deliverer. You are the strength of my life and I trust in You! You are my shield and my mighty Savior, my stronghold of safety and my refuge of peace. I will call upon You, Lord, You are worthy to be praised and exalted! Yours, O Lord, is the greatness, the power, and the glory, the victory, and the majesty forever! For all that is in heaven and in the earth is Yours; it's all Your kingdom and You are exalted and reign as head over all. I recognize that both riches and honor come from You and You have given me power and might and You have made me great and granted me strength!

I love You, Lord! I seek you diligently and I always find You. And I find that gold, revenue, silver, riches, and honor are with You and come from You. You walk with me in the way of righteousness and the paths of justice so that you may cause me the one who loves you to inherit wealth and You want to fill my treasuries.

Scripture References: 2 Sam. 22:1-4, 1 Chron. 29:11-12, Prov. 8:17-21

End of Drought Declaration

Father, in the Name of Jesus, this is the year of God's Glory and I come into agreement with your Word and what the prophets have spoken. I proclaim the End of Drought in my life, my family, my work, and my church! I declare that I hear the Sound of the abundance of rain and it is pouring on me and into every area of my life. It's the end of drought in my family life, my home life, my relationships, my spouse, and my children! It's the end of drought in my finances! My job and everything I set my hand to is blessed! It's the end of drought in my Spiritual life and my natural life. Abundance is invading me in my Spirit, my Soul, and my Body!

I call in the abundance of rain and the fruit that it brings to me! I declare, according to Joel chapter 2, that I am GLAD because of the rain of the Spirit that God gives to me faithfully and I am FULL and OVERFLOW with the New Wine of the Spirit and His anointing oil. I am also FULL and OVERFLOW with BLESSINGS because you bring me into prosperity! You have brought me into a plentiful rain whereby You confirm your inheritance to me and You, Oh God, have provided from ALL Your goodness. RESTORATION is mine! All the years that have been eaten and consumed by the locust and canker worm are RESTORED and MULTIPLIED back to me. My God has dealt wondrously with me. I have plenty. I am satisfied. I praise the Name of my God and I will NEVER be put to shame.

I am BLESSED because I trust in the Lord and my hope is in Him. I am firmly planted and my roots draw from the source of ALL supply, the living waters, and I DO NOT FEAR when heat comes. In dry times I'm not bothered, I'm not anxious, I'm not worried about a thing and I will always continue to flourish and produce fresh, delicious fruit in every season. For the Lord my God, He is the source of ALL supply that I trust in and I stand in strong faith upon Him! God is my Healer, my protector, and my rear guard. My soul is ALWAYS satisfied, my bones are strengthened, and I am like a watered garden, and like a spring of water, whose waters do not fail. I am called one who builds, raises up, repairs, and restores and God's hand is upon me and His favor is with me. I boldly declare that DROUGHT IS OVER and ABUNDANCE IS HERE!

I am SO glad and I blossom abundantly with Joy and Singing. All shall see the glory of the LORD, the Excellency of our God! The end of drought means that the eyes of the blind are opened and the ears of the deaf are unstopped; the lame leap like a deer and the tongue of the dumb sing; waters burst forth in the wilderness and streams in the desert. The parched ground is now a pool and the once thirsty land is now springs of water. This is a picture of my life, Spiritually, Naturally, and Bodily!

Scripture References: Joel 2:23-26, 1 Kings 18:41, Jer. 17:7-8, Isaiah 35:1-8; 58:8-12, Ps. 68:6-11

Open Heaven Declaration

Father God, I thank You that THE HEAVENS ARE OPEN UNTO ME this day! This is a glorious year, a year of HEAVEN ON EARTH! OPEN HEAVEN means MIRACLES, HEALINGS, BLESSINGS, OUTPOURINGS, and DELIVERENCE! Your blessings have come upon me and they OVERTAKE me daily. I am truly blessed in everything I put my hand to and every place I go. According to your covenant promises, You grant to me plenty of goods, You increase every area of my life, and I am fruitful, productive, healthy, and blessed! My God, You have OPENED to me Your GOOD TREASURE, THE HEAVENS are open, and THIS IS MY SEASON of blessing, supply, abundance, and overflow! Because of this and according to Galatians 3:14, the blessing of Abraham has come upon me and, just like him, I am a blessing! You have made me a blessing! I lend, and I give, and I don't need to borrow. I am Abraham's seed and an heir according to the same covenant promises you gave to him.

According to your covenant promise, and Your Word unto me, Lord, I have PROVEN that you have OPENED unto me the windows of HEAVEN, and You have POURED out FOR ME such a blessing that I have to make more room to receive it ALL into my life. ALL that you intend to pour out on me! The devourer is REBUKED for my sake and he cannot and will not destroy the fruitfulness in my life, in Jesus Name! Everyone, even other nations, calls me blessed and sees God's hand of blessing in my life and I am a delight. Today, I SHOUT for joy and I am glad! I am walking in and abiding in every good and perfect gift that you have for me, which comes down from the Father of Lights. Heaven, upon me and all that are with me! I continually say, "Let the Lord be magnified", because it is He who takes great pleasure in the blessing and prosperity of His servant. I am Your servant!

Scripture References: Deut. 28:1-12, Ps. 35:27, Malachi 3:10-12, Gal. 3:13-14, 29, James 1:17

Prayer of Praise

O, magnify the Lord with me and let us exalt His name together! Let the words of my mouth and the meditation of my heart be acceptable in your sight, O Lord, my firm and impenetrable rock and my redeemer!

I will worship toward Your holy temple and praise Your Name because of Your loving-kindness, Your truth, and Your faithfulness; for You have exalted Your Word and Your Name above ALL else and have magnified Your Word above ALL Your Name!

I will bring an offering of praise and thanksgiving to honor and glorify You, and my mouth will be filled with Your praise ALL the day. My lips shall praise You for Your loving-kindness is better than life; so, I will bless You while I live and I will lift up my hands in Your Name!

Scripture References: Ps. 19:14; 34:3; 50:23; 63:3-4; 71:8; 138:2

I Will Give Thanks

I am giving thanks always, for all things, to God the Father in the name of our Lord Jesus Christ. Now thanks be to God, who always leads me in triumph in Christ, and through me, diffuses the fragrance of His knowledge in every place. Thanks be to God, who gives me the victory through our Lord Jesus Christ. I rejoice always and pray without ceasing; in everything I give thanks for this is the will of God in Christ Jesus for me. I enter His gates with thanksgiving and a thank offering and enter His courts with praise. I am thankful to Him and I bless and praise His Name, for He is good and His mercy and loving-kindness are everlasting and His faithfulness and truth endure to all my generations! I will bless the Lord at all times and His praise and thanks shall continually be in my mouth. My soul shall make its boast in the Lord and it will make those around me glad. I magnify and exalt the Lord and as I seek Him, He delivers me from all my fears. I will love You, Oh Lord my strength. You are my rock, and my fortress, and my deliverer. You are my God and my strength and I will trust you. You are my shield and the horn of my salvation, my stronghold. I will call upon You, Lord, You are worthy to be praised and so shall I be saved from my enemies!

Scripture References: Ps. 18:1-3; 34:1-4; 100:4-5, Eph. 5:20, 1 Cor. 15:57, 2 Cor. 2:14, 1 Thess. 5:16-18

My Identity "In Christ"

In Christ, I am not condemned as I walk in His Spirit, for the law of the Spirit of life **in Christ** Jesus has made me free from the law of sin and death. I am justified freely by His grace through the redemption that is **in Christ** Jesus and I will completely fulfill my part in the Body of Christ! I am completely sanctified **in Christ** and called with all the Saints in the Church by Jesus, who became for me, wisdom from God and righteousness, and sanctification, and redemption and I am made alive **in Christ**! I am established and anointed **in Christ** and I thank God who always leads me in triumph **in Christ**, and through me diffuses the fragrance of His knowledge in every place. Every veil over my mind has been taken away and **in Christ**, I am a new creation; old things have passed away; behold, all things have become new. God was and is **in Christ**, reconciling the world to Himself, not imputing their trespasses to them and has committed to me the word of reconciliation, not condemnation.

In Christ, I have liberty and as a Son/Daughter **in Christ,** through faith, I will not judge or discriminate because there is neither Jew nor Greek, there is neither slave nor free, there is neither male nor female. For we are all one **in Christ** Jesus and neither circumcision nor uncircumcision avails anything, but faith working through love and a new creation!

In Christ, I am blessed with every spiritual blessing and I have been raised up together with all the Saints, and we have been made to sit together in the heavenly places! I am His workmanship, created **in Christ** Jesus for good works, which God prepared beforehand that I should walk in them. I have been brought near by the blood of Christ. **In Christ**, I am a fellow heir, of the same body, and a partaker of His promise in Christ through the gospel and I am forgetting those things which are behind and reaching forward to those things which are ahead as I press toward the goal for the prize of the upward call of God **in Christ** Jesus.

In Christ, I will give thanks in everything; for this is the will of God for me and with the faith and love which are **in Christ** I will walk in the exceedingly abundant grace of our Lord. He saved me and called me with a holy calling, not according to my works, but according to His own purpose and grace, which was given to me **in Christ** Jesus before time began and I Hold fast to the pattern of sound words in the faith and love which are **in Christ** Jesus. I am strong in the grace that is **in Christ** Jesus and I abound in the fruit and knowledge of our Lord Jesus Christ so I will be neither barren nor unfruitful.

Scripture References: Rom. 3:35; 8:1-2; 12:5, 1 Cor. 1:2, 30; 15:22, 2 Cor. 1:21; 2:14; 3:14; 5:17, 19, Gal. 2:4; 3:26, 28; 5:6; 6:15, Eph. 1:3; 2:6, 10, 13; 3:6, Phil. 3:13-14, 1 Thess. 5:18, 1 Tim. 1:14, 2 Tim. 1:9, 13; 2:1, 2 Peter 1:7-8

My Identity "In Him"

In Him I live my life, and that life is the light of men and **In Him**, I live and move and have my being. For I am His offspring and for me, all the promises of God **in Him** are Yes, and **in Him** Amen, to the glory of God through me! For He made Him who knew no sin *to be* sin for me, that I might become the righteousness of God **in Him.**

In Him, He chose me before the foundation of the world, that I should be holy and without blame before Him in love. That in the dispensation of the fullness of the times, He might gather together in one all things in Christ, both which are in heaven and which are on earth—**in Him**. And I am found **in Him**, not having my own righteousness, which *is* from the law, but His righteousness, that which *is* through faith in Christ, the righteousness which is from God by faith.

In Him I will walk, having received Him, being rooted and built up **in Him** and established in the faith, just as I have been taught and abounding in it with thanksgiving. **In Him** dwells all the fullness of the Godhead bodily; and I am complete **in Him**, who is the head of all principality and power.

In Him the love of God is perfected in me and I keep His word and know that I abide **in Him** and walk as He walked and His light is shining in me and through me! I have an anointing from the Holy One and I know all things! As I abide **in Him** I don't even need anyone to teach me because that anointing that I have received from Him teaches me concerning all things and is true, and is not a lie, and just as it has taught me, I will abide **in Him**.

In Him I am a child of God and I am purified just as He is purified. Jesus was manifest to take away my sins and **in Him** there is no sin and I abide **in Him** and do not sin. I know that I abide **in Him**, and He in me, because He has given me of His Spirit. **In Him** I have this confidence; that if I ask anything according to His will, He hears me. And if I know that He hears me, whatever I ask, then I know that I have the petitions that I have asked of Him. And I know that the Son of God has come and has given me this understanding, that I may know Him who is true; and that I am **in Him** who is true, in His Son Jesus Christ. This is the true God and eternal life.

Scripture References: John 1:4, Acts 17:28, 2 Cor. 1:20; 5:21, Eph. 1:4, 10, Phil. 3:9, Col. 2:6-7, 9, 10; 1 John 2:5-6, 8, 20, 27; 3:2-3, 5, 6; 4:13, 5:14-15, 20

This Is Who "I Am"

I am forgiven, justified, sanctified, saved by grace, through faith, and I am a new creature in Christ Jesus!

I am a partaker of His divine nature, a son/daughter of God, led by the Spirit of God, and a child of the living God!

I am redeemed from the hand of the enemy, redeemed from the curse of the law, delivered from the powers of darkness, and conveyed into the kingdom of the Son of His love!

I am an overcomer by the blood of the Lamb and the word of my testimony, not moved by what I see, walking by faith and not by sight, and I bring every thought into captivity to the obedience of Christ!

I am strong in the Lord and in the power of His might and I can do all things through Christ who strengthens me, because greater is He that is in me than he that is in the world.

I am an heir of God and a joint heir with Jesus Christ and an heir to the blessings of Abraham, blessed coming in and blessed going out, above only and not beneath and blessed with every spiritual blessing in the heavenly places in Christ.

I am the righteousness of God in Christ and more than a conqueror, healed by His stripes, with all my needs supplied by Christ Jesus and the Lord is the strength of my life.

I am casting all my cares on Jesus because He cares for me and casting down vain imaginations and every high thing that exalts itself against the knowledge of God, being transformed by the renewing of my mind and Christ Jesus is made unto me wisdom from God.

I am taking my authority over all the power of the enemy and I always triumph in Christ Jesus and I am strong and carry out great exploits because I know my God.

I am an imitator of Christ Jesus and I have an anointing from the Holy One and I know all things because that anointing abides in me and teaches me concerning all things.

Scripture References: Deut. 28:6, 13, Ps. 27:1; 107:2, Dan. 11:32, Luke 10:19, Rom. 5:9; 8:14, 16, 17, 37; 12:1-2, 1 Cor. 1:30; 6:11, 2 Cor. 2:14;

4:17-18; 5:7, 21; 6:18; 10:4-5, Gal. 3:13-14, Eph. 1:3; 2:8; 5:1; 6:10, Phil. 4:13, 19, Col. 1:13-14, 1 Peter 2:24; 5:7, 2 Peter 1:4, 1 John 2:20, 27; 4:4, Rev. 12:11

Corporate Prayer

Father, we come before You to worship You and declare that You alone are God, and You alone are worthy of all praise and all glory. You who created the heavens and the earth have determined the end from the beginning and have created us for this time. We know that you have kept us for such a time as this. We surrender our hearts to the Lordship of Jesus Christ and declare our Allegiance to Him alone. We receive the fullness of the Father's love and purpose in our lives and acknowledge that we were bought with a precious price, the Blood of Jesus, and have been set apart for Your work in this, Your appointed time.

We come into agreement with Your prophetic words spoken over us, that Your Apostolic, double-portion anointing is upon us. We declare Your Word, Father, that divine appointments and strategic encounters will release the recognition of Your call in the hearts of all those who are called to partner with us in Your work. We lift them up to You, Father, and stand in agreement that we will see the fruit of Your call in them, in our Body, and in our land. We are a prophetic Body in which Your Rhema is being planted deep in the rich soil of our hearts. We thank You that Your word will not return to You void and it will accomplish that which You have purposed and sent it to do. We declare that we are a people who stand, determined to see the glory of God in our land.

We answer Your call upon us individually and corporately. You have spoken through Your Servants that the time of awakening is at hand and we commit to be a people of effective, fervent prayer, to pray Your will into this earth. We declare according to Your word that we are the spearhead of

Your awakening in our region and we will strike the blow that brings the fullness of Your promise to our land and into our lives. We are called to change the atmosphere over our area and to see heaven come to earth. You have positioned us in this place and have given us this territory to conquer for Your glory and inheritance. You have called us to hewn out wells which we did not dig, and to reap from vineyards and olive trees which we did not plant. We call forth the blessings and the fruition of the prayers of Your people to be manifested in this time. We are a people whose hearts burn with a revival fire for our cities and we have the authority to gain the keys we need for the release of its inhabitants. We walk in the wisdom of God and are not ignorant of the devices of the enemy. We call for the revelation of the plans of the enemy over our cities and declare that we will wield the Sword of the Spirit in our mouths and see his plans come to naught. We thank You that You are making known through us the fellowship of the mystery, to the intent that now the manifold wisdom of God might be made known, by the church, to the principalities and powers in the heavenly places according to the eternal purpose which You accomplished in Christ Jesus our Lord. We will see the thrones of iniquity in our cities overthrown and God's covenant plan for our territory flourish in the days ahead.

We are a covenant people who walk in love and experience the unity of the Spirit in our midst. We are a people of like mind and like beliefs who walk led by the Spirit of God. Our words are edifying to ourselves and to our brethren. We will stand with one another and see the promises of God fulfilled in our lives and in the lives of the people of our region. We thank You, Holy Spirit, that You lead us into all truth and teach us about things to come. We thank You for the anointed word that comes forth in this place to prepare us for Your call. We recognize that we are a people called to worship. We decree that the floodgates of worship are open and that the new song of the Spirit that comes from heaven to earth will go out from us to water the seeds and the plants in the hearts of Your people, that they will bear much fruit. We are a local gathering with an international reach and we decree that the prayers and proclamations that go forth from this place will impact the nations.

We are a Holy Ghost hospital that experiences the power of God's freedom on behalf of all those that You send to us and we experience the power of God in our midst. You have positioned Your gifts in our Body to train us up for the work of the ministry. We declare that none will be left behind and that all will fulfill their divine purpose, call, and destiny. There will be many Apostles, Pastors, Prophets, Evangelists, and Teachers borne out of us to reach the unsaved. Together, we are making a demand on the hidden treasure that God has placed in His people and it is causing everyone to go forth and do great exploits.

Scripture References: 2 Sam. 23, 2 Cor. 9:8, Eph. 3:10

Corporate Word Confession

Father, we join our faith to pray for each other and for ourselves... "For this reason [seeing the greatness of this plan by which we are built together in Christ], we bow our knees before the Father of our Lord Jesus Christ, For Whom every family in heaven and on earth is named [that Father from Whom all fatherhood takes its title and derives its name]. May You grant us out of the rich treasury of Your glory to be strengthened and reinforced with mighty power in the inner man by the [Holy] Spirit [Himself indwelling our innermost being and personality]. May Christ through our faith [actually] dwell (settle down, abide, make His permanent home) in our hearts! May we be rooted deep in love and founded securely on love. That we may have the power and be strong to apprehend and grasp with all the saints [God's devoted people, the experience of that love] what is the breadth, and length, and height, and depth [of it]; [That we may really come] to know [practically, through experience for ourselves] the love of Christ, which far surpasses mere knowledge [without experience]; that we may be filled [through all our being] unto all the fullness of God [may have the richest measure of the divine Presence, and become a body wholly filled and flooded with God Himself]! Now to You, Who by (in consequence of) the [action of Your] power that is at work within us, are able to [carry out Your purpose and] do superabundantly, far over, and above all that we [dare] ask or think [infinitely beyond our highest prayers, desires, thoughts, hopes, or dreams] - To You be glory in the church and in Christ Jesus throughout all our generations forever and ever. Amen (so be it)." (Eph. 3:14-21 Amplified)

"For this reason we also, from the day we heard of it, have not ceased to pray and make [special] request for us, [asking] that we may be filled with the full (deep and clear) knowledge of Your will in all spiritual wisdom [in comprehensive insight into the ways and purposes of God] and in understanding and discernment of spiritual things - That we may walk (live and conduct ourselves) in a manner worthy of the Lord, fully pleasing to You and desiring to please You in all things, bearing fruit in every good work and steadily growing and increasing in and by the knowledge of God [with fuller, deeper, and clearer insight, acquaintance, and recognition]. [We pray] that we may be invigorated and strengthened with all power according to the might of Your glory, [to exercise] every kind of endurance and patience (perseverance and forbearance) with joy, Giving thanks to You, Father, Who has qualified and made us fit to share the portion which is the inheritance of the saints (God's holy people) in the Light. [You, Father] have delivered and drawn us to Yourself out of the control and the dominion of darkness and have transferred us into the kingdom of the Son of Your love, In Whom we have our redemption through His blood, [which means] the forgiveness of our sins." (Col. 1:9-14 Amplified)

"[Let our] love be sincere (a real thing); [Let us] hate what is evil [loathe all ungodliness, turn in horror from wickedness], but hold fast to that which is good. [Help us] Love one another with brotherly affection [as members of one family], giving precedence and showing honor to one another. [May we] Never lag in zeal and in earnest endeavor; be aglow and burning with the Spirit, serving the Lord. [We will] Rejoice and exult in hope; be steadfast and patient in suffering and tribulation; be constant in prayer. [We will] Contribute to the needs of God's people [sharing in the necessities of the saints]; pursue the practice of hospitality. [We will] Bless those who persecute us [who are cruel in their attitude toward us]; [We will] bless and not curse them. [We will] Rejoice with those who rejoice [sharing others' joy], and weep with those who weep [sharing others' grief]. [We commit to] Live in harmony with one another; to not be haughty (snobbish, high-minded, exclusive), but readily adjust ourselves to [people, things] and give ourselves to humble tasks. Never overestimating ourselves or being wise in our own conceits. [We will] Repay no one evil for evil, but take thought for what is honest and proper and noble [aiming to be above reproach] in the sight of everyone. If possible, as far as it depends on us, [We will] live at peace with everyone." (Rom. 12:9-18 Amplified)

Declare: As for me, my house, and my church, we will serve the Lord!

Chapter 3
THE POWER OF YOUR WORDS

Personal Study Notes & Nuggets

In this chapter I have provided scriptures, definitions, and comments designed to foster revelation from the Holy Spirit and a personal discovery of your true design as, what I call, a Speaking Spirit! Your words carry creative life and power to change the environment and circumstances around you. Just as God **spoke** everything into existence in the beginning, we carry the power of life (and death) in our tongues, voices, or mouths. I encourage you to read the scriptures out loud as you follow along with my study.

Matthew 12:37

37 For **by your words** you will be justified and **by your words** you will be condemned.

- Words will justify us or condemn us.

- Words will liberate us or captivate us.
- Words will heal us or make us sick.
- Words will create or destroy.
- Words we spoke yesterday made today.
- Words we speak today make tomorrow.

"Those who say they <u>can</u> and those who say they <u>can't</u> are both right!"

Unknown Author

Proverbs 18:21

21 Death and life are in the **power** of the tongue and those who love it will eat the fruit of it.

Power translates as **YAD** in Hebrew, which means an open hand, to reach or to grasp. The hand can be the creative tool of the body, fashioning, forming, or the instrument of destruction and death.

Notice that the word **power** is likened unto a creative tool the hand uses to fashion or form. God has given us power in our lives to create or re-create our sphere of life and everything that pertains to it. The choice is ours each time we open our mouths; **LIFE** or **DEATH**, Creation or Destruction. There is no middle ground.

God's word that is conceived in your heart and spoken out of your mouth becomes a spiritual force, releasing the ability of God within you and affecting the environment around you!

Unknown Author

The Spoken Word of God

Let's examine our creative beginning and review what God said and how He said it while He was fashioning and forming the universe as we know it. I have abbreviated some of the verses in order to highlight specific thoughts, but it is important to recognize that the inspired scripture begins each creative instance with **"God said"**. His creative action and the resulting manifestation were released by His speaking!

Genesis 1:1, 3, 6, 9, 11, 14, 20, 24, 26

1 In the beginning God **created** the heavens and the earth.

3 Then **God said**, "Let there be light"; and there was light.

6 Then **God said**, "Let there be a firmament in the midst of the waters, and let it divide the waters from the waters."

9 Then **God said**, "Let the waters under the heavens be gathered together into one place, and let the dry land appear"; and it was so.

11 Then **God said**, "Let the earth bring forth grass, the herb that yields seed, and the fruit tree that yields fruit according to its kind, whose seed is in itself, on the earth"; and it was so.

14 Then **God said**, "Let there be lights..."

20 Then **God said**, "Let the waters abound..."

24 Then **God said**, "Let the earth bring forth the living creature..."

26 Then **God said**, "Let Us make man in Our image..."

GOD SPOKE SPECIFICS! He spoke to and told each item in His imagination what to do, how it should act, and where it should land and He gave it all life and expression through His verbal action. If a picture is worth a thousand words, then the images we see in and from our inspired imaginations, minds, and hearts are just waiting to be given clear vocalization, backed by creative power!

Hebrews tells us that everything that is visible was created from the invisible realm through spoken words and faith. Faith (believing) produces things of substance from our dreams (hopes) and imaginations when coupled with our voices. Mix what you say with faith!

Hebrews 11:1-3

1 Now **faith** is the **substance** of **things hoped for**, the **evidence** of **things not seen**.

2 For by it the elders obtained a good testimony.

3 By faith we understand that **the worlds were framed by the <u>word</u> of God** (Word = Rhema, the spoken Word), so that **the things which are seen were not made of things which are visible**.

Let me say it another way... God created with His words, coupled with faith and hope to give them substance and make them evident, all coming from the unseen realm into the seen or visible realm! Faith is the power behind the words and hope is the dream, visual, or image of what is to become visible. All that we see was created by the spoken word of God; it came from an invisible source. We can't see the faith or the words, but they create and they have power! Everything we see or that is visible was made from or came from the invisible or unseen. Let's continue in Hebrews.

Hebrews 1:3

3 who being the brightness of His glory and the express image of His person, and upholding all things by the <u>**word**</u> **of His power** (Word = Rhema, the spoken Word), when He had by

Himself purged our sins, sat down at the right hand of the Majesty on high...

I want you to see this. He didn't say the power of His word, meaning that his word has some power, but the word of His power, meaning His power is in His word. **His power is in what He says!**

Luke 1:37-38

37 For with God **nothing will be impossible**.

38 Then Mary said, "Behold the maidservant of the Lord! Let it be to me **according to your word**." And the angel departed from her.

Literally, it will not be impossible with God to fulfill His every declaration (spoken word)! Since this is a double negative (not impossible) it is easier to say that it **IS possible** with God to fulfill His **EVERY** declaration.

The Amplified Bible says it this way... "For with God nothing is ever impossible and no word from God shall be without power or impossible of fulfillment!" Oh, I like that!

Another way that I like to convey this message is to proclaim that **ONE WORD FROM GOD CHANGES EVERYTHING!** Think about that... just one message or instruction from the Lord, just one prophetic Word or hearing the voice of the Holy Spirit, one simple inspiration or direction from God can put everything in perspective, settle you, establish you, bring peace in trouble and strength in weakness to set you on a victory course that will change everything in you, concerning you, and around you! That is POWERFUL!

What about Our Words?

Matthew 12:34-37

34 Brood of vipers! How can you, being evil, speak good things? For **out of the abundance of the heart the mouth speaks**.

35 A good man out of the good treasure of his heart **brings forth good things**, and an evil man out of the evil treasure **brings forth** evil things.

36 But I say to you that for every idle word men may speak, they will give account of it in the Day of Judgment.

37 For by your words you will be justified, and by your words you will be condemned.

Creating good things, creating evil things! The word "things" means the creation of substance, circumstances, life, death. **What I say today creates tomorrow!**

1.   Words with Grace!

Luke 4:18-22

18 The Spirit of the Lord is upon Me, because He has anointed Me to preach the gospel to the poor; he has sent Me to heal the brokenhearted, to proclaim liberty to the captives and recovery of sight to the blind, to set at liberty those who are oppressed;

19 To proclaim the acceptable year of the Lord.

20 Then He closed the book, and gave it back to the attendant and sat down. And the eyes of all who were in the synagogue were fixed on Him.

21 And He began to say to them, "Today this Scripture is fulfilled in your hearing."

22 So all bore witness to Him, and marveled at **the gracious words which proceeded out of His mouth**. And they said, "Is this not Joseph's son?"

      GRACIOUS translates as **CHARITOS** from the root **CHARIS** which means; Life giving, beneficial, liberating, divinely inspired, creating joy and pleasure.

Colossians 4:6

6 **Let your speech** always be with **grace** *(Chariti, root Charis)*, seasoned with salt, that you may know how you ought to answer each one.

Ephesians 4:29

29 Let no corrupt word proceed out of your mouth, **but what is good for necessary edification**, that it may **impart grace** *(Charin, root Charis)* **to the hearers.**

WORDS WITH GRACE OR GRACE-FILLED WORDS BUILD UP, STRENGTHEN, AND EDIFY!

Ecclesiastes 10:12

12 The words of a wise man's mouth are **gracious** *(favor, pleasant, precious, kind)*, but the lips of a fool shall swallow him up;

2. Words of Spirit and Life!

John 6:63

63 It is the Spirit who gives life; the flesh profits nothing. The **words** *(Rhema)* **that I speak** to you are **spirit** *(Pneuma = God breathed)*, and they are **life** *(Zoe = God's life)*.

3. Eternal Words!

John 6:68

68 But Simon Peter answered Him, "Lord, to whom shall we go? You have the **words of eternal life**."

4. Creative Word Application!

Mark 3:3, 5

3 And **He said to the man** who had the withered hand, "Step forward."

5 And when He had looked around at them with anger, being grieved by the hardness of their hearts, **He said to the man**, "Stretch out your hand." And he stretched it out, and his hand was restored as whole as the other.

Mark 5:41

41 Then He took the child by the hand, and said to her, "Talitha, cumi," which is translated, "Little girl, **I say to you,** arise."

John 5:8

8 **Jesus said to him**, Rise, take up your bed and walk."

John 11:41-43

41 Then they took away the stone from the place where the dead man was lying. And Jesus lifted up His eyes and said, **"Father, I thank You that You have heard Me**.

42 And **I know that You always hear Me**, but because of the people who are standing by I said this, that they may believe that You sent Me."

43 Now when He had said these things, **He cried with a loud voice**, "Lazarus, come forth!"

JESUS SPOKE IN FAITH (Verses 41, 42)

5.   The Book of Acts

Acts 14:8-15

8 And in Lystra a certain man without strength in his feet was sitting, a cripple from his mother's womb, who had never walked.

9 This man heard Paul speaking. **Paul, observing him intently and seeing that he had faith to be healed,**

10 **said with a loud voice**, "Stand up straight on your feet!" And he leaped and walked.

11 Now when the people saw what Paul had done, they raised their voices, saying in the Lycaonian language, "The gods have come down to us in the likeness of men!"

12 And Barnabas they called Zeus, and Paul, Hermes, because he was the chief speaker.

13 Then the priest of Zeus, whose temple was in front of their city, brought oxen and garlands to the gates, intending to sacrifice with the multitudes.

14 But when the apostles Barnabas and Paul heard this, they tore their clothes and ran in among the multitude, crying out

15 and saying, "Men, why are you doing these things? **We also are men with the same nature as you**, and preach to you that you should turn from these useless things to the living God, who made the heaven, the earth, the sea, and all things that are in them,"

Acts 9:34

34 **And Peter said** to him, "Aeneas, Jesus the Christ heals you. Arise and make your bed." Then he arose immediately.

Acts 3:6-8

6 **Then Peter said**, "Silver and gold I do not have, but what I do have I give you: In the name of Jesus Christ of Nazareth, rise up and walk.

7 And he took him by the right hand and lifted him up, and immediately his feet and ankle bones received strength.

8 So he, leaping up, stood and walked and entered the temple with them-- walking, leaping, and praising God.

Psalm 64:1-4

1 **Hear my voice, O God**, in my meditation; preserve my life from fear of the enemy.

2 Hide me from the secret plots of the wicked, from the rebellion of the workers of iniquity,

3 **Who sharpen their tongue like a sword**, and bend their bows to shoot their arrows - **bitter words**,

4 That they may shoot in secret at the blameless; suddenly they shoot at him and do not fear.

WORDS ARE CONTAINERS; THEY WILL CARRY FAITH OR FEAR, BLESSING OR BITTERNESS!

Chapter 4
WORD CONSCIENCE

What Am I Saying?

I want to walk with awareness about what I am saying... before I say it, as I'm speaking it, and after it has been spoken! To actually think about the impact my words are having on my world!

THINK ABOUT WHAT YOU WANT TO SAY, BEFORE YOU SAY IT! GIVE YOURSELF TIME TO ADJUST OR RADICALLY ALTER YOUR WORDS FOR GOOD AND FOR BLESSING SINCE THEY WILL RADICALLY ALTER YOUR LIFE!

You choose your words when you talk to your boss, but do you keep that conscious guard active all the time?

Our MIND plays a major part in the words we speak...

Philippians 4:8

"8 Finally, brethren, whatever things are true, whatever things are noble, whatever things are just, whatever things are pure, whatever things are lovely, whatever things are of good report, if there is any virtue and if there is anything praiseworthy - **meditate** *(think, take inventory, run through or roll over)* **on these things**."

THE THINGS WE ARE THINKING ABOUT OR ARE OCCUPIED WITH IN OUR MIND AND THOUGHTS WILL, MANY TIMES, DETERMINE THE WORDS WE USE WHEN WE TALK! Negative thoughts = Negative Words. Positive thoughts = Positive Words!

Colossians 3:2

2 **Set your mind** on things above, not on things on the earth.

THIS IS OUR DAILY DECISION, WE HAVE TO DECIDE CONSTANTLY!

Our minds are different than a T.V. Turn to channel 2 and its stays on 2 until you turn to channel 4. Our minds are constantly FLIPPING channels; we have to take control and SET IT!

2 Corinthians 10:3-5

3 For though we walk in the flesh, we do not **war** (contend, fight at in the military) according to the flesh.

4 For the weapons of our warfare are not carnal but mighty in God for pulling down strongholds,

5 casting down **arguments (imaginations, thoughts)** and every **high thing (elevated place or barrier)** that exalts itself against the knowledge of God, bringing **every thought (perception, intellect, disposition, purpose, mind)** into captivity (lead away captive) to the obedience of Christ,

CAPTURE THE THOUGHTS, CONTROL THE WORDS!

Guard Your Tongue!

Psalm 34:13

13 **Keep your tongue** from evil, and your lips from speaking deceit.

KEEP YOUR TONGUE, GUARD IT, WATCH IT; SET A FENCE AROUND IT WITH A GATE, A SURVELENCE CAMERA, AND A MONITOR. WATCH WHAT COMES AND GOES!

Psalm 39:1

1 I said, "I will **guard** my ways, **lest I sin with my tongue**; I will **restrain my mouth** with a muzzle, while the wicked are before me."

A MUZZLE IS USED ON A DOG THAT CAN'T KEEP FROM BITING!

Psalm 141:3

3 Set a guard, O LORD, over my mouth; keep watch over the door of my lips.

A GOOD PRAYER TO PRAY EACH DAY!

WORDS ARE LIKE SEEDS, THEY PRODUCE AFTER THEIR OWN KIND. How are you sowing your seeds? We must plant them carefully; seeds that are just thrown on the ground won't produce fruit!

Tour of Proverbs

Proverbs 4:23-24

23 **Keep your heart** with all diligence, for out of it spring the issues of life.

24 **Put away from you** a deceitful mouth, and put perverse lips far from you.

Proverbs 10:19-21

19 In the **multitude of words** sin is not lacking, but he who **restrains his lips** is wise.

20 The **tongue of the righteous** is choice silver; the heart of the wicked is worth little.

21 The **lips of the righteous feed many**, but fools die for lack of wisdom.

Proverbs 12:18-19

18 There is one who speaks like the piercings of a sword, **but the tongue of the wise promotes health.**

19 **The truthful lip shall be established forever**, but a lying tongue is but for a moment.

Proverbs 13:2-3

2 **A man shall eat well by the fruit of his mouth**, but the soul of the unfaithful feeds on violence.

3 He who **guards his mouth** preserves his **life**, but he who **opens wide his lips** shall have **destruction**.

Proverbs 15:28

28 The **heart** of the righteous **studies** how to **answer**, but the mouth of the wicked pours forth evil.

Proverbs 16:23-24

23 The **heart** of the wise **teaches his mouth**, and **adds learning to his lips.**

24 **Pleasant words** are like a honeycomb, **sweetness** to the soul and **health** to the bones.

REMEMBER, YOU'RE THE BOSS, NOT YOUR MOUTH! THE TEACHER RUNS THE CLASS, NOT THE STUDENTS!

LET YOU'RE HEART BE IN CONTROL OF YOUR MOUTH, NOT YOUR HEAD AND YOUR FLESH!

Proverbs 17:27-28

27 He who has knowledge **spares his words**, and a man of understanding is of a calm spirit.

28 Even a fool is counted wise when he holds his peace; when he shuts his lips, he is considered perceptive.

Proverbs 21:23

23 Whoever **guards his mouth and tongue** keeps his soul from troubles.

Proverbs 23:16

16 Yes, my inmost being will rejoice **when your lips speak right things.**

Proverbs 25:11-12

11 **A word fitly spoken** is like apples of gold in settings of silver.

12 Like an earring of gold and an ornament of fine gold is a wise rebuke to an obedient ear.

The Target

Ephesians 4:29-32

29 **Let no corrupt word proceed out of your mouth, but what is good for necessary edification, that it may impart grace to the hearers.**

30 **And do not grieve the Holy Spirit of God,** by whom you were sealed for the day of redemption.

31 **Let** all bitterness, wrath, anger, clamor, and **evil speaking be put away from you, with all malice.**

32 And **be kind to one another**, tenderhearted, forgiving one another, just as God in Christ forgave you.

Ephesians 5:4

4 neither **filthiness, nor foolish talking, nor coarse jesting,** which are not fitting, but rather **giving of thanks**.

Ephesians 5:18-20

18 And do not be drunk with wine, in which is dissipation; but **be filled with the Spirit,**

19 **speaking** to one another in psalms and hymns and spiritual songs, singing and making melody in your heart to the Lord,

20 **giving thanks always for all things** to God the Father in the name of our Lord Jesus Christ.

1 Peter 3:8-10

8 Finally, **all of you** be of one mind, having compassion for one another; love as brothers, be tenderhearted, be courteous;

9 **not returning evil for evil or reviling for reviling** *(Slander, evil speaking)*, but on the contrary **blessing,** knowing **that you were called to this, that you may inherit a blessing.**

10 For "He who would love life and see good days, **let him refrain his tongue** from evil, and his lips from speaking deceit."

Talk About This!

Psalm 77:12

12 I will also meditate on all Your work, and **talk of Your deeds.**

TALK ABOUT GOD! TALK ABOUT WHAT HE IS DOING AND WHAT HE HAS DONE!

Psalm 119:171-172

171 **My lips shall utter praise**, for You teach me Your statutes.

172 **My tongue shall speak of Your word**, for all Your commandments are righteousness.

Psalm 119:172 (New Living)

172 **Let my tongue sing about your word**, for all your commands are right.

Psalm 145:5, 10-12

5 I will meditate **on the glorious splendor of Your majesty**, and **on Your wondrous works**.

10 **All Your works** shall praise You, O LORD, and **Your saints shall bless You**.

11 They shall **speak of the glory of Your kingdom**, and **talk of Your power**,

12 To **make known** *(Boldly proclaim)* to the sons of men **His mighty acts**, and **the glorious majesty of His kingdom**.

Life and Death, Tongue Power!

James 3:1-6

1 My brethren, let not many of you become teachers, knowing that we shall receive a stricter judgment.

2 For we all stumble in many things. **If anyone does not stumble in word, he is a perfect man, able also to bridle the whole body.**

3 Indeed, we put bits in horses' mouths that they may obey us, and we turn their whole body.

4 Look also at ships: although they are so large and are driven by fierce winds, they are turned by a very small rudder wherever the pilot desires.

5 Even so the tongue is a little member and boasts great things. See how great a forest a little fire kindles!

6 And the tongue is a fire, a world of iniquity. The tongue is so set among our members that it defiles the whole body, and sets on fire the course of nature; and it is set on fire by hell."

WHEN WE OPEN OUR MOUTHS AND SPEAK INTO A SITUATION (With faith or belief behind it) WE RELEASE POWER FOR GOOD OR POWER FOR EVIL... BLESSING OR CURSING... LIFE OR DEATH!

Biblical Definitions

BLESS OR BLESSING:

To speak well of, to cause to prosper, to make happy, to invoke goodness upon!

When we pray for people we are using our words and mouth to invoke blessing (health, prosperity, favor, peace, love, joy, marriage...)

CURSE OR CURSING:

The usual biblical meaning is a MALEDICTION!

MAL - Bad, badly, wrong or ill!

DICTION - Manner of expression in words; choice of words!

- Bad manner of expression in words.
- Wrong or bad choice of words.

VERB = A declaration devoted to destruction! Also, to pray against or wish evil against a person, situation, or thing! TO CURSE!

James 3:7-10

7 For every kind of beast and bird, of reptile and creature of the sea, is tamed and has been tamed by mankind.

8 But no man can tame the tongue. It is an unruly evil, full of deadly poison.

9 With it we bless our God and Father, and with it we curse men, who have been made in the similitude of God.

10 <u>Out of the same mouth proceed blessing and cursing. My brethren, these things ought not to be so.</u>

A BIG MOUTH SPEWS CURSING. A LITTLE MOUTH INVOKES BLESSING.

GOD WANTS US TO HARNESS OUR SPEECH (WORDS) AND DIRECT IT TO COME OUT AS BLESSING NOT AS A CURSE!

Matthew 5:44

44 But I say to you, love your enemies, **bless those who curse you**, do good to those who hate you, and **pray for those who spitefully use you and persecute you**,

- USE YOUR WORDS TO COUNTER-ACT THE SITUATION!
- SPEAK BLESSING TO THOSE WHO SPEAK EVIL OF YOU!
- IVOKE GOODNESS UPON, UPLIFT AND ENCOURAGE!

Luke 6:28

28 **bless those who curse you**, and **pray for those who spitefully use you.**

SPITEFULLY - With intent to hurt you (malice), with ill will!

WORDS SPOKEN AGAINST US OR AGAINST OTHERS; HOW DO THEY DAMAGE OR HURT/CURSE?

- Poor self-image (you're ugly, you're dumb, you're stupid)
- Low self-esteem – Thought warfare – Emotional trauma
- Depression – Oppression – Regression
- Anger – Spite – Rage – Bitterness – Unforgiveness – Hate
- Offense – Puts you on the Defensive – Walls

Psalm 109:28

28 Let them curse, **but You bless**; when they arise, let them be ashamed, but let Your servant rejoice.

Psalm 109:28 (Living Bible)

28 Then let them curse me if they like-- I won't mind that if you are blessing me! For then all their efforts to destroy me will fail, and I shall go right on rejoicing!

IF WE CAN TURN A POTENTIALLY DESTRUCTIVE WORD SITUATION WITH BLESSING, THEN WE CAN CONTINUE TO REJOICE, BE HAPPY, AND NOT LOSE OUR JOY! WE ALSO COUNTER-ACT THE POWER OF EVIL WORDS!

Psalm 62:4

4 They only consult to cast him down from his high position; they delight in lies; **they bless with their mouth, but they curse inwardly. Selah (Think or meditate about that!)**

TAKE INVENTORY OF YOUR HEART ATTITUDE WHEN YOU SPEAK GOOD AND BLESS OTHERS! DON'T JUST PUT UP A FRONT OF "NICE WORDS", WHILE THINKING EVIL!

The Living Bible says, "They are so friendly to my face while cursing in their hearts!"

More Definitions

MOUTH - The opening in the head through which food is taken in and sounds are made!

MOUTH OFF - To talk loudly and insultingly, talking back!

BIG MOUTH - A person who talks too much, especially in an opinionated way!

Big Mouth

This is the designation I'm assigning for the unbridled mouth and tongue. CURSING will proceed from it!

Proverbs 15:1-2

1 A soft answer turns away wrath, but **a harsh word stirs up anger.**

2 The tongue of the wise uses knowledge rightly, but **the mouth of fools pours forth foolishness**.

Proverbs 15:28

28 The heart of the righteous studies how to answer, but **the mouth of the wicked pours forth evil.**

Proverbs 10:11

11 The mouth of the righteous is a well of life, but **violence covers the mouth of the wicked.**

Proverbs 10:31-32

31 The mouth of the righteous brings forth wisdom, but **the perverse tongue will be cut out.**

32 The lips of the righteous know what is acceptable, but **the mouth of the wicked what is perverse.**

Little Mouth

By contrast, BLESSING will pour forth!

Proverbs 17:27

27 **He who has knowledge spares his words**, and a man of understanding is of a calm spirit.

Proverbs 10:32

32 **The lips of the righteous know what is acceptable**, but the mouth of the wicked what is perverse.

WE KNOW WHAT IS ACCEPTABLE! WE KNOW WHAT SHOULD BE COMING OUT OF OUR MOUTHS, NOT SIMPLY WHAT CAN COME OUT OF OUR MOUTHS!

Proverbs 12:6

6 The words of the wicked are, "Lie in wait for blood," *(SET A TRAP FOR DEATH)* but **the mouth of the upright will deliver them**.

OUR MOUTHS ARE FOR DELIVERANCE, NOT DECEPTION! FAITH, NOT FEAR!

Proverbs 12:14

14 **A man will be satisfied with good by the fruit of his mouth**, and the recompense of a man's hands will be rendered to him.

Deut. 30:9-19

9 The LORD your God will make you abound in all the work of your hand, in the fruit of your body, in the increase of your livestock, and in the produce of your land for good. For the LORD will again rejoice over you for good as He rejoiced over your fathers,

10 if you obey the voice of the LORD your God, to keep His commandments and His statutes which are written in this Book of the Law, and if you turn to the LORD your God with all your heart and with all your soul.

11 For this commandment which I command you today, it is not too mysterious for you, nor is it far off.

12 It is not in heaven, that you should say, 'Who will ascend into heaven for us and bring it to us, that we may hear it and do it?'

13 Nor is it beyond the sea, that you should say, 'Who will go over the sea for us and bring it to us, that we may hear it and do it?'

14 **But the word is very near you, in your mouth and in your heart**, that you may do it.

15 See, I have set before you today **life and good, death and evil**,

16 in that I command you today to love the LORD your God, to walk in His ways, and to keep His commandments, His statutes, and His judgments, that you may live and multiply; and the LORD your God will bless you in the land which you go to possess.

17 But if your heart turns away so that you do not hear, and are drawn away, and worship other gods and serve them,

18 I announce to you today that you shall surely perish; you shall not prolong your days in the land which you cross over the Jordan to go in and possess.

19 I call heaven and earth as witnesses today against you, that I have set before you life and death, blessing and cursing; **therefore choose life, that both you and your descendants may live!**

Chapter 5

YOU CAN HAVE WHAT YOU SAY

Words of Faith

Romans 10:8-10

8 But what does it say? '**The word is near you, in your mouth, and in your heart**' (that is, the word of faith which we preach):

FAITH IS IN YOUR MOUTH, AND IN YOUR HEART!

9 that if you **confess with your mouth** the Lord Jesus and believe in your heart that God has raised Him from the dead, you will be saved.

10 For with the heart one believes unto righteousness, and **with the mouth confession is made unto salvation**.

THE GREATEST MIRACLE CAME FROM YOU MOUTH!

Mark 11:22-24

22   So Jesus answered and said to them, "Have faith in God. *(Literally, Have the GOD KIND OF FAITH.)*

23   For assuredly, I say to you, **whoever says** to this mountain, 'Be removed and be cast into the sea,' and does not doubt in his heart, but **believes** that those things **he says** will come to pass, **he will have whatever he says**.

YOU WILL HAVE, WHAT YOU BELIEVE? WHAT YOU PRAY? NO, YOU WILL HAVE <u>WHAT YOU SAY</u>!

24   Therefore I say to you, whatever things you **ask** when you pray, believe that you receive them, and you will have them."

YOU HAVE TO SPEAK TO ASK! YOU HAVE TO SAY SOMETHING! IN VERSE 23: BELIEVE IS USED ONLY 1 TIME, WHILE SAY IS USED 3 TIMES! <u>SAY</u> - SPEAK, DECLARE, TALK, ASK, COMMAND, SHOUT!

CREATE THINGS WITH YOUR MOUTH; SAY, BELIEVE, HAVE!

Luke 17:6

So the Lord said, "If you have faith as a mustard seed, **you can say** to this mulberry tree, 'Be pulled up by the roots and be planted in the sea,' **and it would obey you**.

Luke 17:6 (New Living)

"...Your command would bring immediate results!"

Matthew 17:20

So Jesus said to them, "Because of your unbelief; for assuredly, I say to you, if you have faith as a mustard seed, you will say to this mountain, 'Move from here to there,' and it will move; and nothing will be impossible for you."

THE POWER OF WHAT YOU SAY IS UNLIMITED!

WHAT MOUNTAIN NEEDS TO BE MOVED? POSITIVE OR NEGATIVE, JESUS APPLIED IT TO SICKNESS, DISEASE, DEMONS, DEATH, STORMS (NATURE: WIND, WAVES, WEATHER), FIG TREE, WATER/WINE. JESUS SPOKE TO THOSE MOUNTAINS!

The 3 Voices That Talk To You

1.   The voice from the pit cries out when cancer, diseases, sickness, fear, blindness, troubles, and pain try to come into your life saying, "You're sick!" "You're in trouble!" "You're hurtin' for certain!"

2.   The voice from God, His Spirit, and His Word says to us, "By His stripes you are healed!" "He bore our sickness and pain!" "He took our curse, being made a curse for us!" "My God shall supply all your need according to His riches in glory by Christ Jesus!" All the promises that SAY something to us...

SO, SYMPTOMS, SICKNESS, AND DISEASE SAY ONE THING TO US AND GOD SAYS ANOTHER THING. THE POINT IS...

3.   YOUR VOICE. WHAT ARE YOU GOING TO SAY ABOUT IT? YOU HAVE SOMETHING TO SAY! WHOSE SIDE ARE YOU GOING TO TAKE WITH YOUR WORDS? ARE YOU GOING TO SAY WHAT THE DEVIL AND THE WORLD SAYS, OR WHAT GOD SAYS?

THIS MUCH IS TRUE: WHAT YOU SAY, IS WHAT YOU BELIEVE, IS WHAT YOU HAVE!

Joel 3:10

"...let the weak say, 'I am strong.'"

- **LET THE SICK SAY, I AM HEALED!**
- **LET THE TROUBLED SAY, I AM DELIVERED!**
- **LET THE OPPRESSED SAY, I AM FREE!**

NOTICE HOW THE POWER OF YOUR WORDS IS DIRECTLY CONNECTED TO ACTIVATED FAITH.

Matthew 9:20-22

20 And suddenly, a woman who had a flow of blood for twelve years came from behind and touched the hem of His garment.

21 **For she said to herself**, 'If only I may touch His garment, **I shall be made well**.'

22 But Jesus turned around, and when He saw her He said, "Be of good cheer, daughter; **your faith has made you well**." And the woman was made well from that hour.

Mark 7:24-30

24 From there He arose and went to the region of Tyre and Sidon. And He entered a house and wanted no one to know it, but He could not be hidden.

25 For a woman whose young daughter had an unclean spirit heard about Him, and she came and fell at His feet.

26 The woman was a Greek, a Syro-Phoenician by birth, and **she kept asking** Him to cast the demon out of her daughter.

27 But Jesus said to her, "Let the children be filled first, for it is not good to take the children's bread and throw it to the little dogs."

28 And **she answered and said** to Him, "Yes, Lord, yet even the little dogs under the table eat from the children's crumbs."

29 Then He said to her, "**For this saying** go your way; the demon has gone out of your daughter." **(BECAUSE OF WHAT YOU SAID!)**

30 And when she had come to her house, she found the demon gone out, and her daughter lying on the bed."

Matthew 15:27-28

27 And **she said**, "Yes, Lord, yet even the little dogs eat the crumbs which fall from their masters' table."

28 Then Jesus answered and said to her, "O woman, great is your faith! Let it be to you as you desire." And her daughter was healed from that very hour.

I STARTED THIS SERIES BY SAYING:

- The words we spoke yesterday made today.

- The words we speak today make tomorrow.

THOSE WHO SAY THEY <u>CAN</u> AND THOSE WHO SAY THEY <u>CAN'T</u> ARE BOTH RIGHT!

I AM A COMPOSITE OF WHAT I'VE BEEN SAYING! YOU ARE A COMPOSITE OF WHAT YOU'VE BEEN SAYING; GOOD, BAD, OR INDIFFERENT! IF YOU WANT TO CHANGE, CHANGE WHAT YOU ARE SAYING!

Proverbs 18:21 - Death and life are in the power of the tongue and those who love it will eat the fruit of it.

Speaking Out Of a Renewed Mind!

HAVE YOU EVER: Let words fly out of your mouth, and apologized later (Unjudged, no standard)... wishing you could TAKE BACK WHAT YOU SAID?

"Insert foot in mouth"

"I didn't mean to say that"

"Where did that come from"

Ephesians 4:29 (AMP)

Let no foul or polluting language, nor evil word, nor unwholesome or worthless talk ever come out of your mouth, but **only such speech as is good and beneficial to the spiritual progress of others, as is fitting to the need an occasion that it may be a blessing and give grace (ability) to those who hear it**.

Ephesians 5:4

4 neither filthiness, **nor foolish talking, nor coarse jesting, which are not fitting, but rather giving of thanks**."

Ephesians 5:18-20

18 And do not be drunk with wine, in which is dissipation; but **be filled with the Spirit,**

19 **speaking** to one another in **psalms** and **hymns** and **spiritual songs**, **singing** and **making melody in your heart** to the Lord,

BE FILLED WITH THE SPIRIT, SPEAKING. Of course, the chapter and verse separations are only there for the reader's convenience. So he's saying that our mouth and what we say to each other is connected to being filled with the Holy Spirit! Literally, "Be Being Filled!"

20 **giving thanks always for all things** to God the Father in the name of our Lord Jesus Christ"

John 6:63

63 It is the Spirit who gives life; the flesh profits nothing. **The words that I speak to you are spirit, and they are life**.

Romans 10:9-10

"That if you **confess with your mouth** the Lord Jesus and believe in your heart that God raised Him from the dead, you will be saved. For with the heart one believes to righteousness **and with the mouth confession is made to salvation**."

OUR MOUTH AND OUR CONFESSION ARE VERY IMPORTANT AT THE BEGINNING POINT OF OUR SALVATION, AND THEY CONTINUE TO BE IMPORTANT ALONG ALL OF OUR ETERNAL JOURNEY IN CHRIST!

Romans 12:1-2

1 I beseech you therefore, brethren, by the mercies of God, that you **present your bodies** a living sacrifice, holy, acceptable to God, which is your reasonable service.

2 And **do not be conformed to this world**, but **be transformed by the renewing of your mind**, that you may prove what is that good and acceptable and perfect will of God.

PRESENT YOUR BODIES - That includes the mouth and the tongue, they're part of our bodies!

DO NOT BE CONFORMED TO THE WORLD - Its ways, its thinking, ITS WORDS! But be TRANSFORMED, or changed by God's power and HIS WORDS, his PROVISION! Let God's Word Transform you AND YOUR WORDS!

THE RENEWING OF YOUR MIND - Change your thinking processes; let them be renewed or transformed. As we change the way we view and analyze the world around us, and change our attitudes and motivations, WE CHANGE OUR WORDS!

THEY GO HAND IN HAND. RENEW THE MIND, RENEW THE MOUTH! (Out of the abundance of the heart the mouth speaks!) Since the mind is the organizer of our words... adjusting one, automatically adjusts the other!

HOUSE CLEANING: Not everyone has an overnight house cleaning when they get saved. I mean, if you smoked before you got saved, you may have still smoked. It took, some of us, some time for our life habits, morals, thinking, TALKING, to change, or be renewed.

As we change our thinking (RENEW OUR MINDS) then our morals, habits, actions, AND WORDS WILL ALL CHANGE!

COMPUTER: What we input or program in a computer is what comes out (GIGO). We can alter it, make it bigger, prettier, more organized... but it's still the same info we originally put in. Our minds are similar, WHAT GOES IN, COMES OUT (OF YOUR MOUTH)!

Look at Romans 12:3

"For I say, through the grace given to me, to everyone who is among you, not to think of himself more highly than he ought to think, but to **think soberly**, as God has dealt to each one a measure of faith."

THINK SOBERLY - to be of sound mind, be in right mind!

The same word, sophroneo (so-fron-eh'-o), is used in Mark 5:15 and Luke 8:35 to describe a man who had been demon possessed and had the legion, **"in his right mind!"**

Luke 8:35

35 Then they went out to see what had happened, and came to Jesus, and found the man from whom the demons had departed, **sitting at the feet of Jesus, clothed and in his right mind**. And they were afraid.

Luke 8:29

29 For He had commanded the unclean spirit to come out of the man. For it had often seized him, and he was kept under guard, bound with chains and shackles; and he broke the bonds and was driven by the demon into the wilderness.

Mark 5:3-5

3 ...who had his dwelling among the tombs; and no one could bind him, not even with chains,

4 because he had often been bound with shackles and chains. And the chains had been pulled apart by him, and the shackles broken in pieces; neither could anyone tame him.

5 And always, night and day, he was in the mountains and in the tombs, **crying out** and cutting himself with stones. *(That's crazy!)*

NOT TOO HIGHLY (PROUD, ARROGANT, VAIN), KEEP YOUR MIND IN ITS PLACE, RIGHT MINDED!

Romans 12:16

16 Be of the same mind toward one another. Do not set your mind on high things,

Spiritually Minded

Romans 8:5-7

5 For those who live according to the flesh **set their minds** on the things of the flesh, but those who live according to the Spirit, **(SET THEIR MINDS ON)** the things of the Spirit.

6 For to be carnally minded is death, **but to be spiritually minded is life and peace.**

7 Because the carnal mind is enmity (positive hatred) against God; for it is not subject to the law of God, nor indeed can be."

DEATH AND LIFE ARE IN THE POWER OF THE TONGUE! SOUNDS THE SAME AS THIS PASSAGE!

SET YOUR MIND - DECIDE TO THINK, TAKE CONTROL OF YOUR MIND, BE THE BOSS OF YOUR MIND! TELL IT TO THINK ABOUT GOD, HIS WORD, HIS WAYS, HIS LIFE, AND PEACE!

VERSE 7 - THE CARNAL MIND HAS NO CONSTRAINTS (MORALITY, GOD'S LAW) AND IT CANNOT BE CONSTRAINED. IT IS AGAINST GOD.

Romans 8:11

11 But if the Spirit of Him who raised Jesus from the dead dwells in you, He who raised Christ from the dead will also **give life to your mortal bodies (INCLUDING YOUR MOUTH!)** through His Spirit who dwells in you.

LOOK AT THIS IN CONTEXT... WE HAVE GOD'S HELP THROUGH HIS INDWELLING SPIRIT! CALL ON GOD'S INGRAFTED, IMPLANTED, LIVING HELP!

1 Corinthians 2:16

16 For 'who has known the mind of the Lord that he may instruct Him?' But **we have the mind of Christ**.

[The mind of Christ] The views, feelings, and temper of Christ. We are influenced by his Spirit.

WE HAVE CHRIST'S MIND, GOD'S THOUGHTS, BY HIS SPIRIT, ALIVE INSIDE OF US! WE CAN DRAW FROM HIS MIND, HIS THINKING, AND HIS WAYS; CONSULTING CHRIST! HAVE A TALK WITH GOD! WE CAN ACTUALLY THINK LIKE JESUS IS THINKING! OUR MOUTH AND SPEECH WILL FOLLOW SUIT!

Hebrews 8:10

10 For this is the covenant that I will make with the house of Israel after those days, says the Lord: **I will put My laws in their mind and write them on their hearts**; and I will be their God, and they shall be My people.

IT'S OUR COVENANT RELATIONSHIP WITH GOD; HIS LAWS, HIS THOUGHTS, HIS MORAL JUDGEMENT, HIS WISDOM HAS BEEN GIVEN TO US, PUT IN OUR MINDS, WRITTEN ON OUR HEARTS! WE CAN CULTIVATE IT OR NEGLECT IT!

WHEN YOU PLANT A SEED IN THE GARDEN, YOU MUST WATER IT, IT NEEDS SUNLIGHT, GOOD SOIL, AND TENDING...

Philippians 2:1-8

1 Therefore if there is any consolation in Christ, if any comfort of love, if any fellowship of the Spirit, if any affection and mercy,

2 fulfill my joy **by being like-minded**, having the same love, being of one accord, **of one mind**.

3 Let nothing be done through selfish ambition or conceit, but in lowliness of mind let each esteem others better than himself.

4 Let each of you look out not only for his own interests, but also for the interests of others.

5 **Let this mind be in you** which was also in Christ Jesus,

YOUR MIND WANTS TO WANDER; IT'S PRONE TO PRIDE. KEEP IT IN CHECK, SET IT ON GOD, WASH IT, RENEW IT, CHANGE IT! "...I've changed my mind..."

6 who, being in the form of God, did not consider it robbery to be equal with God,

7 but made Himself of no reputation, taking the form of a bondservant, and coming in the likeness of men.

MAKE YOUR MIND A SERVANT OF GOD!

8 And being found in appearance as a man, He humbled Himself and became obedient to the point of death, even the death of the cross."

MAKE YOUR MIND OBEY YOU AND BECOME OBEDIENT TO GOD'S WORD.

2 Timothy 1:6-7

6 Therefore I remind you to stir up the gift of God which is in you through the laying on of my hands.

7 For God has not given us a spirit of fear, but of power and of love **and of a sound mind**."

GOD GAVE US THE SPIRIT LIVING IN US OF A SOUND, A STABLE MIND! WE CAN SPEAK OUT OF THAT MIND! AS WE KEEP OUR MINDS DAILY WASHED, SET, RENEWED, ESTABLISHED; OUR WORDS WILL COME FORTH FROM THAT WELL SPRING OF SWEET WATER - THAT WATER OF OUR WORDS WILL REFRESH AND STRENGTHEN ALL WHO DRINK OR HEAR!

Psalm 77:12

12 I will also **meditate on all Your work, and talk of Your deeds**.

Proverbs 15:23

23 **A man has joy by the answer of his mouth, and a word spoken in due season, how good it is**!

1 Peter 3:10

10 For "He who would love life and see good days, **let him refrain his tongue from evil, and his lips from speaking deceit**.

Quick References and Information

Matthew 15:10-11 - Defile means to make unclean or pollute; to stain or spot

Matthew 15:18 - HEART = mind, will, and emotions

Matthew 12:34b-36 - Good treasure, Evil treasurer - Room, Vault, Container

G.I.G.O. - We must guard our hearts (Vault)

You are the GATE/DOOR KEEPER of what enters the mind and what comes out the mouth.

James 3:2-12 - Bridle our tongues/Harness them with the Word of God. THOUGHTS SPAWN WORDS!

2 Corinthians 10:3-5 - Cast down Arguments, Vain imaginations, Accusations, Pride, Self-will, Immoral, Lies

- **Bring every thought captive - Hold it in check to the Word/Spirit**
- **The Word is our standard or ruler to measure with**

Romans 12:2 - Renew the mind - a good treasurer - wash

2 Timothy 1:7 - God has not given us a spirit of fear but... A SOUND MIND.

1 Corinthians 2:16 - We have the mind of Christ.

Philippians 2:5 - Let this mind be in you which was also in Christ Jesus.

FINAL WORDS...

I believe that you are entering into the fullness of your identity and destiny! This is YOUR time! This is YOUR season of blessing, increase, freedom and joy! I pray Great Grace upon you and everything that concerns you! Remember, Life is too short not to have FUN!

If this book or any part of it has been a help or blessing to you, please contact me to let me know. I want to hear your testimony of God's manifest Goodness in your life!

CONTACT INFORMATION

If you would like more in-depth information or materials by David R. White on teaching, training, prayer or leading worship, please visit our website or email us:

Website: www.newsong.cc

Email: newsong@newsong.cc

New Song Worship Center

P.O. Box 2202, Costa Mesa, CA 92628

36672677R00044

Made in the USA
San Bernardino, CA
27 May 2019